The Dedalus Press
13 Moyclare Road
Baldoyle
Dublin 13
Ireland

www.dedaluspress.com

The poems here collected originally appeared in two separate
Dedalus Press publications. *The Wild Marketplace* (Dedalus Press,
1985) and *For the Living and the Dead* (Dedalus Press, 1994),
a "collaborative effort' between Tranströomer and Deane.

ISBN 978 1 906614 53 9

Dedalus Press titles are distributed in North America by
Syracuse University Press, Inc., 621 Skytop Road,
Suite 110, Syracuse, New York 13244,
and in the UK by
Central Books, 99 Wallis Road, London E9 5LN.
UK representation, Inpress Books: www.inpressbooks.co.uk
Cover image © iStockphoto.com / oriontrail

The Dedalus Press receives financial assistance from
The Arts Council / An Chomhairle Ealaíon

INSPIRED NOTES

Poems of Tomas Tranströmer

Comprising poems from the two volumes
The Wild Marketplace
and *For the Living and the Dead*

Translated by
John F. Deane

DEDALUS PRESS
DUBLIN, IRELAND

CONTENTS

⤍

Translator's Note / 7

⤍

The Wild Marketplace

FOR THE LIVING AND THE DEAD

TRANSLATOR'S NOTE

TOMAS TRANSTRÖMER WAS BORN in 1931 and grew up in Stockholm. The author of fifteen collections of poetry, since 1967 he has lived in Vasteras where he worked as a psychologist. In 1954 he published his first collection—*17 Dikter*—which placed him at once in the forefront of contemporary Swedish poetry. He has given many readings of his work throughout the world (in Dublin in 1985 on the publication of his collection, *The Wild Marketplace,* the text of which is included here), and a large selection of his poems was published by Ecco Press in America in 1987, edited by Robert Hass. There is also an edition of his work in translation by Robin Fulton from Bloodaxe Books. Indeed, Dedalus published Fulton's translation of *The Sorrow Gondola (Sorgegondolen)* in 1997 as the first in its Poetry Europe series of publications.

Tranströmer is no stranger to receiving major prizes for his poems, including the Petrarch Prize, the Bonnier Poetry Prize, the Pilot Prize and the prestigious Nordic Prize. In 2011 he received the Nobel Prize for Literature for poems of "condensed, translucent images" which give us "fresh access to reality".

"My poems," Tranströmer has said, "are meeting places. Their intent is to make a sudden connection between aspects of reality that conventional languages and outlooks generally keep apart. Great and small details of the landscape meet, divided cultures and people merge in a work of art, Nature meets Industry, etc. What looks at first sight like a confrontation turns out to be a connection."

The power of the poetry serves to explore those deeply important elements of life ordinarily incapable of conscious control. Hence the poems tend towards a mystic strain without any of the overt implications of the term 'religious'. And the poems show a growing emphasis on truth-telling, a totally honest faithfulness to the poet's individual and verifiable experience.

"When I started writing, at sixteen," Tranströmer says, "I had several like-minded friends at school. At times, when the classes seemed too boring, we passed notes to each other across our desks, poems, aphorisms, which returned with the more or less enthusiastic comments of the other. What an impression those scribbles made! Now there is the fundamental situation of poetry. The lessons of life go rumbling by. We send one another our inspired notes."

—John F Deane

The present publication collects the poems from two previous books published by the Dedalus Press, namely *The Wild Marketplace* (1985) and *For the Living and the Dead* (1994).

The Wild Marketplace

DET VILDA TORGET

Short Pause in the Organ Recital

The organ stops playing and there is deathly silence in
    the church but only for a few seconds.
So the faint humming passes through from the traffic
    outside, the greater organ.

And we are surrounded by the mumbling of traffic that
    wanders round along the cathedral's walls.
There glides the outside world like a transparent film
    and with shadows struggling in pianissimo.

As if entering among the sounds from the street I hear
    one of my pulses beating in the silence,
I hear the circulation of my blood, the cascade that is
    concealed deep within me, that I go around with;

and as near to me as my blood, and as far away as a
    memory from a four-year-old
I hear the long-distance truck go by, causing the six-
    hundred-year-old walls to tremble.

It is here as unlike a mother's embrace as anything can
    be, still I am a child right now
who hears the adults chatting far away, the voices of
    profit and loss mingling with each other.

On the blue benches sits a sparse congregation. And
    pillars rise like curious trees;
without roots (except for the common floor) and
    without crowns (except for the common ceiling.

I reanimate a dream. That I am standing in a church-
    yard alone. Everywhere the heather gleams
as far as the eye can see. For whom am I waiting? A friend.
And why does he not come? He is already here.

Slowly death turns up the light from below, from the
    ground. The heath gleams all intense lilac—
no, in a colour no-one has seen … until morning's pale
    light comes in through the eyelids.

And I waken to that immovable PERHAPS, that carries
    me through the wavering world.
And every abstract picture of the world impossible as a
    blueprint of a storm.

At home the all-knowing Encyclopedia stood, a full
    meter on the shelf, I learned to read from it.
But every person has his own encyclopedia written
    down, it grows out of every soul,

it is written from birth onwards, the hundreds of
    thousands of pages stand pressed against each other,
and still with air between them! like the quivering leaves
    in a forest. Book of contradictions.

What is standing there changes every moment, the
    pictures touch themselves up, the words glisten.
    A surge rolls through the whole text, that is followed
    by the next surge, and the next ….

From March '79

Tired of all who come with words, words but no language,
I went to the snow-covered island.
The wild does not have words.
The unwritten pages spread themselves out in all
    directions!
I come xxx across the marks of roe-deer's hooves in the
    snow.
Language but no words.

Memories Watch Me

A morning in June when it's too early yet
to wake, and still too late to go back to sleep.

I must go out through greenery that's crammed
with memories, that follow me with their eyes.

They are not visible, wholly dissolve
into background, perfect chameleons.

They are so close that I can hear them breathe
although the singing of birds is deafening.

Winter's Gaze

I tilt like a ladder and reach in
with my face to the second floor of the cherry tree.
I am within the bell of colours rung by the sun.
The dark red berries I consume faster than four magpies.

Then I am smitten suddenly by the cold from a long
    distance.
The moment turns black
and remains fixed like the marks of an axe in a bole.

From now onwards it is late. We take ourselves off
    halfrunning
out of sight, down, down in the antique sewage system.
Tunnels. Where we wander about for months,
half on duty and half in flight.

Brief devotions when some shutter opens up above us
    and a weak light falls.
We look upwards: the starry firmament through the
    sewer grating.

The Station

A train has rolled in. Carriage after carriage stands,
but no doors open, no-one gets off or on.
Are there no doors to be found at all? In there it is
    crowded
with locked-in people who are moving to and fro.
They are staring out through the immovable windows.
And outside a man goes along the train with a hammer.
He smites on the wheels, which toll faintly. Except right
    here!
Here the ringing swells incomprehensibly: a thunderclap,
a cathedral-bells-sound, a world-circumnavigating-sound,
that lifts the whole train and the neighbourhood's wet
    stones.
Everything is singing. You will remember this. Proceed.

Answer to a Letter

In the bottom drawer I hit upon a letter which originally came twenty-six years ago. A letter in a panic, which continues to pant when it arrives for the second time.

A house has five windows; through four of them the day shines bright and still. The fifth faces onto a dark sky, thunder and storm. I am standing by the fifth window. The letter.

Occasionally a chasm widens between Tuesday and Wednesday but twenty-six years can pass in a moment. Time is not a straight line stretching ahead, but rather a labyrinth, and if you press yourself against the walls in the right place you can hear the hurrying steps and voices, you can hear yourself going past, there on the other side.

Did the letter receive an answer at any time? I don't remember, it *was* a long time ago. The countless thresholds of the waves have continued to wander. The heart continuously took its leaps from second to second, like the toad in the wet grass of August.

The unanswered letters are heaped up in a pile, like cirrostratus-clouds foreboding storms. They keep on weakening the sunbeams. Sometime I shall answer. Sometime when I am dead and lean at last concentrate. Or at least so far away from here that I can discover myself again. When I am newly arrived in the great city, on 125th Street, in the wind on the street of dancing garbage. I who love to stroll and vanish among the crowds, a letter T in the unending masses of texts.

The Icelandic Hurricane

Not a shuddering of the earth but a skyquake. Turner could have painted it, firmly lashed down. A single glove whirled past just now, many kilometres from its hand. I shall make my way along against the wind to that house on the other side of the field. I am flickering in the hurricane. I am being X-rayed, my skeleton is handing in its resignation. Panic grows while I cross, I founder, I founder and drown on dry land! What a burden it is, all I have to drag along suddenly, what a burden for the butterfly to take a barge in tow! Arrived at last. A final wrestling with the door. And inside now. Inside now. Behind the big pane of glass. What a strange and magnificent idea glass is—to be close without being struck. Outside a horde of transparent sprinters of gigantic shape is rushing by over the plateau of lava. But I no longer founder. I sit behind the glass, still, my own portrait.

The Blue Anemones

To be bewitched—nothing is more simple. It is one of the oldest tricks of spring and of the fields: the blue anemones. They are, in a way, unexpected. They shoot up out of last year's brown rustling in disregarded places where a glance would otherwise never fall. They burn and hover, yes precisely hover, and that is due to their colour. That ardent violet-blue colour has nowadays no weight at all, but with a low ceiling. "Career"—irrelevant! "Power" and "publicity"—ridiculous! They arranged, no doubt, a great reception up in Nineveh, they maked rute and mickle bang. High ceilings—above all those crowns hung crystal chandeliers like vultures made of glass. Instead of such an overdecorated and noisy cul-de-sac the blue anemone open an underground passage to the true festival, which is dead silent.

The Blue House

It is a night of radiant sun. I stand in the dense forest and gaze towards my house with its haze-blue walls. As if I had recently died and was seeing the house from a new angle.

It has stood for more than eighty summers. Its wood is impregnated with four times joy and three times sorrow. When someone who has lived in the house dies, it is repainted. The dead person himself paints, without a brush, from within.

On the other side there is open terrain. Formerly a garden, now grown wild. Stagnant breakers of weeds, pagodas of weeds, texts springing up, upanishads of weeds, a viking fleet of weeds, dragon heads, lances, weed empire!

Over the wild garden flutters the shadow of a boomerang that is thrown time and again. It has a connection with one who lived in the house long before my time. Almost a child. An impulse flows out from him, a thought, a volition: "Create ... draw ..." In order to escape his fate.

The house resembles a child's sketch. A vicarious childishness that developed because someone too early abandoned the task of being a child. Open the door, come in! In here there is agitation in the roof and peace in the walls. Over the bed hangs an amateur painting, showing a ship with seventeen sails, hissing wave crests and a wind which the gilded frame can not restrain.

It is always so early inside here, it is before the fork in the road, before the irrevocable moment of choosing. Thank you for this life! All the same, I lack alternatives. All outlines want to become actual.

A motor far away on the water draws out the summer horizon. Both joy and sorrow swell in the magnifying glass of the dew. We don't really know it, but suspect it: there exists a sister ship to our life, which goes a wholly other shipping route. While the sun is on fire behind the islands.

Satellite Eyes

The earth is rough, no mirror.
Only the coarsest spirits
can be reflected there: the Moon
and the Great Ice Age.

Come nearer in the dragon haze!
Heavy clouds, thronging streets.
A soughing rain of souls.
Barrack yards.

Nineteen Hundred and Eighty

He glances fitfully over the newspaper page.
Feelings come, so chilled they're taken for thoughts.
Only in deep hypnosis could he be his other I,
his hidden sister, the woman who goes with the
    hundred thousand
screaming "Death to the Shah!"—though he is
    already dead—
a marching black tent, pious and full of hate.
Jihad! Two who shall never meet take charge of
    the world.

Black Picture Postcards

1

The almanac written up, future unknown.
The cable hums its folksongs without a homeland.
Snowfall on the lead-still sea. Shadows
    grappling on the wharf.

2

In the midst of life it happens that death will come
taking the measurements of man. The visit
is forgotten, life goes on. But the costume gets
    sewn in the silence.

Firescribbling

During the dismal months, my life sparkled only when
    I made love with you.
As the firefly ignites and then goes out, ignites, goes out
    —one can follow its flight by glimpses
in the dark night among the olive trees.

During the dismal months the soul sat shrunken and
    lifeless,
but the body took the straight path to you.
The night sky bellowed.
By stealth we milked the cosmos and survived.

Many Steps

The icons are laid in the earth with their faces upwards
and the earth is trampled down
by wheels and shoes, by thousands of steps,
by ten thousand doubters' heavy steps.

In dreams I stepped down into a luminous pond under
    the earth,
a swelling liturgy.
What a powerful longing! What idiotic hope!
And over me the trampling of millions of doubters.

Postlude

I drag like a grapnel over the bottom of the world.
Everything that I don't need gets caught.
Tired indignation, burning resignation.
The Executioners gather stones, God is writing in
    the sand.

A silent room.
The furniture stands ready for flight in the moonlight.
I go slowly into myself
through a forest of hollow suits of armour.

Dream Seminar

Four billion people on the earth.
And they all sleep, they all dream.
In every dream faces crowd in, and bodies—
the people dreamed of more numerous than us.
But they take up no space ...
It may happen you fall asleep at the theatre.
Right in the middle of the play your eyelids drop.
The double exposure of a short moment: the scene
in front of you is outflanked by a dream.
At length the scene exists no more, it is you.
The theatre in the most honest depths!
The mystery with the overwrought
theatre director.
The perpetual new rehearsals ...
A bedroom. It is night.
The sky is dark and flowing through the room.
The book that someone fell asleep from
is still there opened out
and lying wounded on the bed's edge.
The eyes of the sleeper stir,
they follow the text that has no letters
in another book—
illuminated, oldfashioned, swift.
A dizzying commedia that is inscribed
inside the eyelids' monastery walls.
A sole exemplar. There it is right now!
It is, in the morning, altogether erased.
The mystery of that great extravagance!
Obliteration ... As when the tourist is stopped

by suspicious men in uniform—
they open his camera, unroll his film
and allow the sun to kill the pictures:
so dreams are blackened out by the light of day.
Obliterated, or just invisible?
There is an out-of-sight dreaming
always in progress. Light for other eyes.
A zone where creeping thoughts can learn to walk.
Faces and figures become re-grouped.
We move on a street, among people
in the blazing sun.
But just as many or more
whom we do not see
are there inside dark buildings
that rise on either side.
Sometimes one of them appears at the window
and glances down at us.

Codex

Men of footnotes, not of headlines. I find myself in the
    deep corridor
that would have been dark
if my right hand did not shine like a pocket torch.
The light falls on something written on the wall
and I see it
as the diver sees the name of the sunken hull shimmering
towards him in the flooding depths:
ADAM ILEBORGH 1448. Who?
He who made the organ spread out its lumpish wings
    and rise—
it held itself hovering for nearly a minute,
What a successful experiment!
Written on the wall: MAYONE, DAUTHENDEY, KAMINSKI…
    The light falls on name after name.
The walls are completely scrawled upon.
They are the almost obliterated names of artists,
people of footnotes, the unplayed, the half-forgotten,
    the immortal unknown.
For just a moment it feels as if all of them are
    whispering their names at the same time —
whisper added to whisper making a breaker that comes
    headlong down the corridor
without knocking anybody down.
And yet it is no longer a corridor.
Nor a burial ground nor a market square but a little of
    both.
It is a greenhouse too.
Here there are heaps of oxygen.

The dead of the footnotes can breathe deeply, they are
    included in the ecological system as before.
But there is a great deal that they escape!
They escape swallowing the morality of might,
they escape the black-and-white chequered game where
    the stench of corpses is the only thing that never dies.
They are rehabilitated.
And those who are no longer able to receive
    have not ceased to give.
They unrolled a little of the brilliant and melancholy
    Gobelin tapestry
and then they lost their grip.
Some are anonymous, they are my friends
but I don't know them, they are like those stone people
that are found cut out on gravefinds in old churches.
Mild or stern reliefs on walls we graze against, figures
    and names
hollowed into stone floors, on the way to obliteration.
But those who really want to be stricken off the list...
They do not remain in the region of footnotes,
they enter the downward tending career that ends in
    oblivion and peace.
In total oblivion. It is a sort of examination
that is taken in silence: to go over the frontier without
    anyone noticing ...

Carillon

Madame despises her guests because they are willing to
    stay at her shabby hotel.
I have the corner room on the first floor: a wretched
    bed, a bare bulb in the ceiling.
Peculiarly enough, heavy drapes where a quarter of a
    million invisible mites are on the march.

A street for pedestrians passes outside
with its sluggish tourists, nimble schoolchildren, men in
    work clothes who push their rattling bikes.
Those who think they make the earth go round and those
who think they go helplessly round in the grip of the earth.
A street where we all walk, and where does it emerge?

The single window of the room looks onto something else:
The Wild Marketplace,
an area of ferment, a great tremulous surface, at times
    full of folk and at times deserted.

What is inside me materializes there, all terrors, all
    expectations.
All the inconceivable that will yet occur.

I have low beaches, if death steps up two decimetres
    I am submerged.
I am Maximilian. The year is 1488. 1 am held under
    lock and key here in Bruges
because my enemies are bewildered—
they are evil idealists and what they did in the backyard
    of horrors I can not describe, I cannot transform
    blood into ink.

I am also the man in overalls who pulls his clattering
    bike along down on the street.
I am also the one who is seen, the tourist who moves
    and halts, moves and halts
and lets his gaze wander over the moontanned pale faces
    and billowing stuff of the old paintings.

No one determines where I shall go, least of all myself,
    although each step is where it has to be.
To walk about in the fossil wars where all are
    invulnerable because all are dead.

The dusty masses of leaves, the walls with their
    apertures,
the garden walks where petrified tears are crackling
    under one's heels …

Unexpectedly, as if I had stepped against a tripwire, the
     bellringing in the anonymous tower is set off.
Carillon! The sack bursts open at its seams and the
     tones roll out over Flanders.
Carillon! The cooing iron of the bells, hymn and street-
     ballad, all in one, and written trembling on the air,
The doctor with trembling hand writes out a
     prescription that no one can decipher but the
     handwriting is recognized ...

Over steeple and square, grass and grain
bells are ringing for living and slain.
Between Christ and Antichrist hard to attend!
The bells will fly us all home in the end.

They have gone silent.

I am back in the hotel room: the bed, the light, the
     hangings. Curious sounds can be heard, the cellar
     dragging itself upstairs.

I am lying on the bed with my arms spread out.
I am an anchor that has dug its way down carefully and
     is holding fast
the enormous shadow floating up above
the great unknown I am a part of and which is surely
     more important than I.

Outside the pedestrian way goes by, the street where my steps die away and also what has been written, my foreword to silence, my psalm turned inside out.

Molokai

We stand on the slope and far below us the roofs of
    leper colony gleam.
The downhill incline we could manage but we'll never
    have time to get up the slope before dark.
Therefore we turn back through the forest, going
    among trees with their long blue needles.
Here is silence, it is a silence like that when the hawk is
    coming.
It is a forest that will pardon everything but forgets
    nothing.
Damien, out of love, chose life and oblivion. He won
    death and renown.
But we see these events from the wrong direction: a heap
of stones instead of the sphinx's face.

NOTES

'The Blue Anemones'
The phrase here translated as "they maked rute and mickle bang" is, in the original "the giordo rusk ok mykit bangh"—and is a quotation from a medieval Swedish text. The blue anemone is the "anemone hepatica", common in Sweden, Finland, Russia, associated with the coming of Spring.

'Codex'
Codex = manuscript. Ileborgh and Mayonc are old, masters of the organ; Kaminski, a German speech composer; and Dauthendey, a German writer who died in 1918.

'Carillon'
Carillon = the pealing of bells. The poem is situated in Bruges in the Autumn of 1982. Maximilian, later Kaiser Maximilian 1, was imprisoned in Bruges in 1488 and his followers executed.

'Molokai'
One of the islands in the Hawaii group, best known for its leper colony where Father Damien worked and died some 100 years ago.

For the Living and the Dead

FÖR LEVANDE OCH DÖDA

The Forgotten Captain

We have many shadows. I was on my way home
one September night when Y
after forty years climbed up out of his grave
and kept me company.

At first he was a total blank, a name merely
but his ideas swam
more quickly than time could run
and caught us up.

I put his eyes to my eyes and saw
the ocean of war.
The last boat he sailed
materialized beneath us.

Ahead, astern, ships of the Atlantic convoy crept,
the ones that would survive
and the ones that bore The Mark
(invisible to everyone)

while sleepless days took over from one another
but never did from him—
his life-jacket bulged under his oilskin.
He never did come home.

An internal weeping made him bleed to death
in a hospital in Cardiff.
He could, at last, lay himself down
and be transformed to a horizon.

Farewell eleven-knot convoys! Farewell 1940!
Here ends the history of the world.
The bombers were left hanging on the air.
The heather-covered moors came into bloom.

A photo from the beginning of this century shows a strand.
Six well-dressed boys stand there.
They have sailing-boats in their arms.
And my! What grave expressions!

Boats that became life and death for some of them.
And to write about the dead—
that is another game that will grow ponderous
with what is yet to come.

Six Winters

1

In the dark hotel a child is sleeping.
Outside: the winter night
where the great-eyed dice are rolling.

2

An elite of the petrified dead
in Katarina Churchyard
where the wind shivers in its armour from Svalbard.

3

A winter of war where I lay ill
grew an immense icicle outside the window.
Neighbour and harpoon, memory without explanation.

4

Ice hangs down from the edge of the roof.
Icicles: the Gothic, turned upside down.
Abstract cattle, udders of glass.

5

On a side-track an empty railway wagon.
Still. Heraldic.
Journeys in its claws.

6

Night snowhaze, moonlight. The jellyfish of the moon
floats above us. Our smiles
as we head homeward. Avenue bewitched.

The Nightingale in Badelunba

In the green midnight at the nightingale's northern boundary. Heavy leaves hang in a trance, the deaf motorcars rush towards the neon-line. The voice of the nightingale does not step aside, it is as penetrating as the crowing of a cock, but lovely, and without vanity. I was in prison and it visited me. I was sick and it visited me. I wasn't aware of it then but I am now. Time streams down from sun and moon and into all the tick-tock, tick-tock-thankful clocks. But just here no time exists. Except for the voice of the nightingale, the raw resounding tones that hone the pallid scythe of the night sky.

Alkaline Reaction

A wood in May. Where my whole life comes haunting:
invisible vanload of furniture. Birdsong.
In the silent pools the midge-larvae
and their frenzied dancing question marks.
I escape to the same places, the same words.
A chill breeze from the sea, the icedragon licks
the back of my neck while the sun is blazing.
The vanload is burning with cool flames.

Berceuse

I am a mummy at rest in the blue coffin of the trees,
in the perpetual soughing of cars and rubber and asphalt.

What happens during the day submerges, the lessons
are heavier than life.

The wheelbarrow rolled out on its single wheel and I
travelled forward on my own whirling psyche, but now
my thoughts have ceased going round and the
wheelbarrow has acquired wings.

At long last, when space has turned black, an aeroplane
will come. The passengers will see cities underneath
them glittering like gothic gold.

Shanghai Streets

The white butterfly in the park is being read by many.
   I love this cabbage butterfly as if it were a fluttering
   corner of truth itself.

At dawn the running crowds jump-start our silent
   planet.
Then the park fills up with people. Each one with eight
   faces polished like jade, for every situation, for
   avoiding blunders.
Each one also with the invisible face that reflects
   "something not to be mentioned".
Something that emerges in weary moments and is rank
   as a draught of viper brandy with its lasting scaly
   aftertaste!

The carp in the pond perpetually move, they swim even
   while they sleep, they are models for the faithful:
   always in motion.

2.

Now it is mid-day. Laundry is fluttering in the grey sea
    winds high above the cyclists
who come in tight shoals. Watch out for the labyrinths
    off to either side!

I am surrounded by written characters I can't decipher,
    I am totally illiterate.
But I have paid as I ought and have receipts for
    everything.
I have collected about me so many illegible receipts.
I am an old tree with withered leaves that are hanging
    on intact and that cannot fall to the ground.

And a breath from the sea causes all these receipts to
    rustle.

3.

At dawn the tramping crowds treadle-start our silent
     planet.
We are all on board the street. It's a crush, like on the
     deck of a ferry.
Where are we going to? Have we enough teacups to go
     round? We may think ourselves fortunate to have
     got on board this street!
It is a thousand years before the birth of claustrophobia.

Behind each of us going about here, there floats a cross
     that will catch us up, overtake us, join with us.
Something that will steal up on us from behind and
     cover our eyes and whisper "guess who this is!"

We almost look happy out in the sun, while we bleed to
     death from wounds of which we are not even aware.

Deep in Europe

I, dark hulk floating between two lock-gates,
rest in bed in the hotel while the city wakens round me.
The quiet clamour and the grey light come streaming in
and lift me softly to the next level: morning.

Horizon overheard. They have something to say, the dead.
They smoke but do not eat, don't breathe but still have
    voices.
Soon I will be hurrying through the streets like one of
    them.
The blackened cathedral, heavy as a moon, causes ebb
    and flow.

Leaflet

Silent fury scribbles inwards on the wall.
Fruit-trees in blossom, the cuckoo calls.
It is spring's narcosis. But silent fury
paints its slogans backwards in the garages.

We see everything and nothing, but straight as periscopes
handled by the shy crew from underground.
It's the minutes' war. The blazing sun
stands over the hospital, suffering's parking-place.

We living nails hammered down into society!
One day we will come loose from everything.
We will know death's air under our wings
and grow milder and wilder than we are here.

The Indoors is Without End

It is 1827, spring. Beethoven
hoists his death-mask and sets sail.

Europe's millstones are grinding on.
The wild geese fly towards the north.

Here is the north, here is Stockholm
hovels and palaces afloat.

The logs in the royal fireplace
collapse from Present Arms to Stand at Ease.

Peace prevails, vaccine, potatoes,
but the city's springs breathe heavily.

Latrine casks in palanquins like paschas
are brought during the night over the North Bridge.

The cobblestones make them stagger
mamselles idlers fine gentlemen.

Inexorably still is the sign-board
with the smoking blackamoor.

So many islands, so many people rowing
with invisible oars against the stream!

The channels open out, April, May
and sweet honey slobbering June.

The heat reaches islands a long way out.
All but one the hamlet doors stand open.

The hand of the serpent-clock licks the silence.
Rock slopes gleam with the patience of geology.

This is the way it happened, more or less.
It's a mysterious family tale

about Erik, bewitched by a curse,
disabled by a bullet through the soul.

He went off to town, met an enemy
and sailed home sick and grey.

He spent all that summer lying at home.
The implements grieving on the walls.

He lies awake, hears the woollen fluttering
of night-flying creatures, his moonlight comrades.

His strength dries up, he thrusts in vain
against the iron-fettered morrow.

And God of the depths cries out of the depths
"Deliver me! Deliver yourself!"

All action turns inwards from the surface.
He's torn apart, put together again.

The wind blows up and the wild dog-rose
clings fast to the fleeing light.

The future opens out, he gazes in
to the self-agitating kaleidoscope

sees vague fluttering faces
of families yet to come.

By mistake his glance hits on me
as I'm going about right here

in Washington, among majestic houses
where only every other pillar carries weight.

White buildings, crematorium style
where the dream of the poor falls into ashes.

The gentle declivity begins to steepen
and imperceptibly turns into a precipice.

Vermeer

No sheltered world … Right behind the wall the noise
     begins
the tavern begins
with laughter and bickering, rows of teeth tears din of bells
     and the disturbed brother-in-law, the death-bringer
     for whom we must all tremble.

The huge explosion and the delayed tramping of rescue

the boats that swagger about in the anchorage, the coins
that crawl down deep in the wrong man's pocket
claim piled on claim
gaping red flower-cups that sweat out premonitions of
     war.

Out from that, straight through the wall into the bright
     atelier
into the second that will live for centuries.
Canvasses that are titled "The Music Lesson"
or "Woman in Blue reading a Letter"—
she's in her eighth month, two hearts kicking within her.
Behind her on the wall a creased-up map of Terra
     Incognita.

Breathe calmly … There is an unknown blue material
     fastened firmly to the chairs.
The golden rivets flew in with unprecedented haste
and stopped dead
as if they were never anything else but stillness.

There is singing in the ears from either depth or height.
It's the pressure coming from behind the wall.
It leaves every fact to hover
and keeps the paint-brush steady.

It hurts to go through walls, you will grow ill from it
but it is necessary.
The world is one. But walls ...
And the wall is a part of your self—
whether or not you know it, it's the same for all
except for little children. For them—no walls.

The clear sky has placed itself a-tilt against the wall.
It's like a prayer to emptiness.
And the emptiness turns its face to us
and whispers
"I am not empty, I am open."

Romanesque Arches

Within the immense romanesque church the tourists
    were crowded together in the half-darkness.
Vault gaping behind vault without any overview.
A few candleflames flickered.
An angel without face embraced me
and whispered through my whole body:
"Don't be ashamed that you are human, be proud!
Within you, vault opens up behind vault ad infinitum.
Never will you be finished, and that's as it ought to be."
I was blind with tears
and shoved out on the sun-simmering piazza
along with Mr and Mrs Jones, Herr Tanaka and Signora
    Sabatini
and within them all vault opened behind vault ad
infinitum.

Epigram

The buildings of capital, the hives of killer bees, honey
    for the few.
There he served his time. But in a dark tunnel he
    unfurled wings
and flew with no one watching. He had to live his life
    all over again.

A Woman's Portrait, 19th Century

The voice is smothered in her clothing. Her eyes
follow the gladiator. Then she herself
stands on the arena. Is she free? A gilt frame
                    constricts the picture.

Medieval Motif

Beneath our enchanting play of features waits
always and ever the skull, the pokerface.
While the sun rolls slowly on across the sky.
                    The chess game proceeds.

A hairdresser's clippers sound from the thicket.
And slowly the sun rolls on across the sky.
The game of chess comes to a halt, it's drawn. In
                              the rainbow's silence.

Airmail

On the hunt for a letterbox
I took the letter through the city.
In the great forest of stone and concrete
fluttered the straying butterfly.

The postage-stamp's flying carpet
the swaying lines of the address
added to my sealed-in truth
right now floating above the ocean.

The Atlantic's creeping silver.
The cloud-banks. The fishing-boat
like a spat-out olive stone.
And the keel-wakes' pallid scars.

Here below the work goes slowly.
I often glance towards the clock.
The tree-shadows are black numerals
in the avaricious silence.

The truth is to be found on the ground
but no-one ventures to carry it off.
The truth is lying on the street.
No-one makes it his own.

Madrigal

I inherited a dark wood to which I seldom go. But a day will come when the dead and the living change places. Then the wood will begin to stir. We are not without hope. The most serious crimes remain unsolved despite the efforts of many policemen. In the same way there exists, somewhere in our lives, a great love, unsolved. I inherited a dark wood but today I am going into another wood, the bright one. Every living thing that sings, wriggles, oscillates and crawls! It is spring and the air is very strong. I have a degree from oblivion's university and am as emptyhanded as the shirt on the clothesline.

Golden Wasp

The blindworm, that legless lizard, courses the length of
    the porch step
quietly majestic as the anaconda, differing only in
    dimensions.
The sky is covered by clouds but the sun squeezes itself
    through. It's that kind of day.

This morning my dear one drove away the evil spirits.
As when the door to a dark storehouse in the south is
    thrown open
and the light floods in
and the cockroaches dart off swiftly swiftly into corners
    and up the walls
and are gone—now you see them, now you don't—
    just so her nakedness made the demons flee.

As if they had never been.
    But they'll be back.
With a thousand hands to disconnect the antiquated
    telephone-exchange of the nerves.

It's July the fifth. The lupins are stretching themselves
    upwards as if wishing to glimpse the ocean.
We are in the church of staying silent, in the wordless
    piety.
As if the unforgiving faces of the patriarchs don't exist,
nor the misspelling, in stone, of the name of God.

I saw a TV preacher, true to name, who had collected
    lots of money.
But now he was weak and needed the support of a
    bodyguard
a well-tailored young man with a smile stiff as a muzzle.
A smile that choked back a scream.
The scream of a child left behind in a hospital bed when
    the parents depart.

The divine touches a person lightly and kindles a flame
    but then withdraws.
Why?
The flame draws shadows to itself, they fly in crackling
    and join the flame
that climbs and blackens. And the smoke spreads out
    black and choking.
In the end only black smoke, in the end only the gentle
    executioner.

The gentle executioner leans forward
over the square and the crowd that form a granulated
    mirror
in which he can see himself.

The greatest fanatic is the greatest doubter. He doesn't
    know it.
He is a pact between two
where one is a hundred percent visible and the other
    invisible.
How I abhor the phrase "a hundred percent."

Those who cannot exist anywhere else except on their
     faces
those who are never absent-minded
those who never open the wrong door and get a glimpse
     of the Unidentified One:
pass them by!

It's July the fifth. The sky is covered by clouds but the
     sun squeezes itself through.
The blindworm courses the length of the porch step,
     quietly majestic as an anaconda.
The blindworm as if the civil service did not exist.
The golden wasp as if idolatry did not exist.
The lupins as if a "hundred per cent" did not exist.

I know the depth where one is both prisoner and
     sovereign, like Persephone.
I often lay in the stiff grass down there
and saw the earth form a vault above me.
The vault of the earth.
Often—that makes half my life.

But today my gaze has abandoned me.
My blindness has gone away.
The dark bat has abandoned my face and is scissoring
     around in summer's bright sphere.

John F. Deane was born on Achill Island in 1943. He founded Poetry Ireland, the national poetry society, and *Poetry Ireland Review* in 1979, as well as the Dedalus Press which he ran for almost twenty years until 2005. He has published several collections of poetry as well as novels and short stories. His many awards and prizes include the O'Shaughnessy Award for Irish Poetry, the Marten Toonder Award for Literature and poetry prizes from Italy and Romania. In 2008 he became the President of the European Academy of Poetry. His latest publications are the poetry collection, *The Eye of the Hare* (Carcanet Press, 2011), and the volume of essays, *The Works of Love* (Columba Press, 2010). He is a member of Aosdána.